Whistling Steam

Romance of Indian Rails

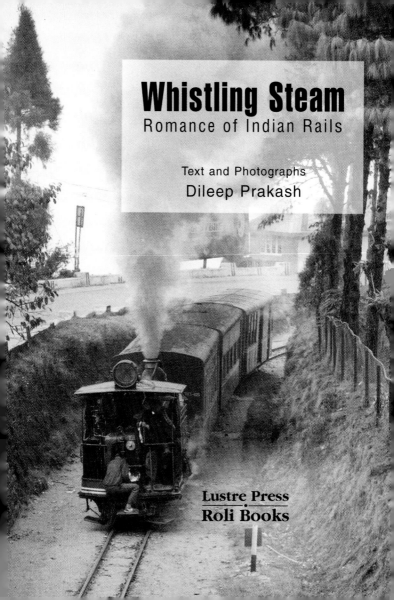

Whistling Steam
Romance of Indian Rails

Text and Photographs
Dileep Prakash

Lustre Press
Roli Books

Ever since the first steam locomotive came to India, we have had an enduring romance with the railway. The iron devil, as the locomotive is called, conjures up visions of a black engine chugging through green fields with smoke billowing from its chimney, trailed by a string of red carriages.

The railway as we know it today is the combination of the steam loco and the metal rails. Even though France and England were experimenting on steam engines in the 1770s, a 'real train' did not move till fifty years later. In 1825, the first passenger train ran between Stockton and Darlington in England. The locomotives were designed by the father-son team of George & Robert Stephenson. Thus was born the famous *Rocket*. In 1830, Stephenson designed the first time-tabled service for the Liverpool & Manchester Railway. In the same year, the first American locomotive, *Best Friend of Charleston*, chugged out on the South Carolina railroad. In 1835, Germany imported a Stephenson-built locomotive, *Adler*, and a driver from England, and ran its first train. Trains were seen in Holland and Italy in 1839 and in 1848 in Spain. The first Russian railway was built at Tsarskoe Selo in 1837, but serious work to link Moscow to St. Petersberg began only in 1842.

Although railway companies were floated by 'glorified blacksmiths' and 'cigar-chewing' entrepreneurs, the railway inspired novelists, artists, musicians and film-makers. Claude Monet spent a year painting the St. Lazare station in Paris. The celebrated work, *Rain Steam and Speed*, by Turner (1843) is now in the National Gallery, London. A century later, Elvis Presley, Bob Dylan and a host of jazz musicians wrote songs on the train theme.

The WP 7015 is shunted out of the Dehradun shed for the Doon Railway Centenary.

While passenger trains were plying in Europe and America, the British brought the first locomotive to India to haul load in 1851. This was a six-wheeled tank engine called *Thomason* and was used on a construction site near Roorkee, Uttar Pradesh. *Thomason* was probably India's only 4.85-ft standard gauge engine and was built by E.B. Wilson. Her life was, however, short-lived – she died when her boiler exploded.

India's second locomotive, *Lord Falkland*, was an unglamorous shunter – an engine used to move carriages between different tracks at the Byculla Yard in Bombay. It was a 5.6-ft broad gauge (BG) engine (the standard in India now) commissioned on 18 February 1853 by Great India Peninsular Railway (GIPR). On 16 April, the country's first passenger train was flagged off from Boribunder in Bombay. Since the train was to carry 400 distinguished guests through a 34-km distance to Thane, GIPR took no chances. It used three engines, the *Sultan*, *Sindh* and *Sahib* bought from Vulcan Foundries. History gets blurred here. All books say three engines hauled the train. But the famous photograph taken by Jamsetjee Jeejeebhoy shows only one engine. Perhaps, two engines were trailing a little behind as back-ups!

The GIPR is mentioned in Jules Verne's *Around The World In Eighty Days*. In 1872, protagonist Phileas Fogg and his French servant Passepartout went on a trip around the world. India was connected from Bombay to Calcutta via the GIPR with a break in between. Yet, the journey was finished in three days. Vernes mentions that the 80-mile (128 km) rail journey from Allahabad to Benares was covered in two hours – an average of 64 kmph. Well, some of our fastest trains today average only about 65 to 70 kmph.

A Wankaner fireman fills the water reservoir of a YP.

Other railway firms were just as ambitious. Take East India Railway which operated from Howrah in Calcutta. In 1855, it shipped two engines from Kiston, Hewitson & Thomson in Leeds. These engines were christened *Express* and *Fairy Queen* 40 years later. *Fairy Queen* has found a place in the Guinness Book as the oldest working locomotive in the world. Its sister, the *Express*, is an exhibit in Jamalpur.

Transporting locomotives by ships was not without mishaps. *HMS Goodwin*, bringing the first railway carriage model, sank and the ship bringing the first locomotives to India was misdirected to Australia! Imported locomotives cost Rs 29,000 apiece in 1885. These engines came completely knocked down and were assembled in India. Manufacturing started in the late 1880s and went on till 1972 when Chitranjan Locomotive Works rolled out the last steam engine, a WG (in the Indian Railways code this refers to broad gauge goods), aptly called *Antim Sitara*. Interestingly, Morvi State Railway in Gujarat, which was the first builder of meter gauge (MG) locomotives in 1871, also saw the last steam train in India 130 years later.

Most countries have one gauge. But India has a non-standard broad gauge – thanks to a compromise between Lord Dalhousie (who favoured a 6-ft gauge) and the Court of Directors who wanted the world standard 4 ft 8.5-in gauge. The meter gauge was also brought in and the hill railways used the narrow gauge track (of 2 ft 6 in and of 2 ft). Locomotives were designed for the specific gauge and traction.

In the early years, railway systems adopted individual standards that resulted in a plethora of engine types. Most early locomotives had six-wheel arrangements in the 2-2-2, 0-4-2 or 2-4-0 type. If that sounds abstruse, it is merely shorthand for denoting the positioning of the wheels in the front, middle and rear. For example, a car is 2-0-2: two wheels in the front, none in the middle, and two at the back. So, if a locomotive is 0-4-2, it means that the middle has four wheels and there are two wheels at the rear.

Maintaining a large variety of locomotives

was a problem and so in the early 1900s, British Engineering Standards Association (BESA) standardised locomotive designs. BESA locomotives for heavy passenger services (HPS) became the standard 'mail' train engine. These designs lasted till the Locomotive Standards Committee came up with six Indian Railway Standards (IRS) classes in 1924. These were the X-class locomotives.

During World War II, locomotives, wagons, and track material were taken from India to the Middle East. Hence, emergency orders had to be placed with American and Canadian manufacturers. Close to 660 locomotives made by the US-based Baldwin Locomotive Works and the Canada Locomotive Co. were imported. The American War Department (AWD) and the Canadian (CWD) types were used in the early years to haul superfasts like *Toofan Mail*. Their satisfactory working influenced the post-war IRS designs, of which the WP 4-6-2 and WG 2-8-2 type locomotives were the most prolific.

While BG could carry heavier loads and was

faster, it was expensive. In 1871, Lord Mayo established the MG to work in areas with limited traffic. The first line from Delhi to Farukhnagar used 'A' class engines. One of them, *Lord Lawrence*, is preserved in Gorakhpur. The MG branch lines were more picturesque and romantic than the BG trunk lines since they passed through unspoilt rural India. Film-maker Satyajit Ray used beautiful steam imagery in his films *Pather Panchali* and *Aparajito*, with both having footage of a steam train running on lesser known branch lines in Bengal and Rajasthan. Today, *The Royal Orient* chugs through the deserts of Rajasthan pulled by post-war meter gauge YGs (meter gauge goods).

An interesting MG machine is the X-class rack engine on the Nilgiri Mountain Railway (NMR) which has a geared wheel to overcome the steep gradient (1:12). The geared wheel runs on a toothed rack between the two rails of the track. Low pressure cylinders drive the geared wheels while high pressure cylinders drive the loco. These engines were built by Schweizerische

Locomotive and Maschinenfabrik, Wintherthur, Switzerland. You can still see them trudging up the Nilgiri slopes. However, the most individualistic of the railways were those that used the narrow gauge (NG). Their classification was also peculiar: some locomotives were known by the names of the lines they worked on – like 'RD' for Raipur Dhamtari line, 'PL' for Parlakimedi line – while some were known by the makers' name, like Bagnall and Sentinel.

The first NG track was built in 1863 for Gaekwar Baroda State Railway (GBSR). But the track was laid too lightly and bullocks pulled the train for ten years! The 96-km Kalka-Shimla NG hill railway ran on engines ordered from North British, UK and Krauss Maffei, Munich. These engines then went to the beautiful Kangra Valley Railway from Pathankot to Jogindernagar. The biggest NG network was the Satpura lines of South Eastern Railway that had some of the most beautiful steam engines. Some of the smallest locomotives to work in India were the Shantipur engines built by WG Bagnall.

The smaller NG, a 2-ft gauge, was restricted to a few lines. One was the Darjeeling Himalayan Railway (DHR) that changed its engines twice, settling finally for the world famous B-class Saddle Tanks in 1889. These work efficiently till today. *Baby Sivok*, a small locomotive built by Orenstien-Koppel, is still on the line, although it is meant only for steam enthusiasts. In West India, Matheran Light Railway (MLR) was a 2-ft line and used engines ordered from Orenstien-Koppel in 1907. Gwalior is the only other haven for the 2-ft gauge. In the 1890s, the Maharaja got his first locomotive built by Brush.

Over the 150 years of history of the steam locomotive, it is difficult to put a definite time frame to the Golden Age of Steam in India. If we look at locomotive types and their physical beauty then the first half of the twentieth century might have been the golden era. In 1950, steam locomotives dominated the world's railways. They were in regular production in 20 countries. Ten years later, things changed:

steam engines were an extinct breed in North America and were in obvious retreat in Europe.

But steam engines reached a high in India in 1963-64 – all of 10,810 steam locomotives. Most prestigious passenger trains were hauled by the X-class and by the post-war, bullet-nosed, WP (broad gauge passenger). The WP pulled 16 coaches comfortably at an average speed of 50-60 kmph. Freight operations were in the able hands of the WG on the broad and YG on the meter gauge. In 1964, *Taj Express* was introduced to allow tourists to visit Agra and return to Delhi the same day. It ran at a whopping 105 kmph with a WP in command!

The logo of the Indian Railways is a steam engine – a steaming X-class pacific. But there are no steams running now. The railways had to modernise. The numbers began to taper off in 1965, and by 1980 only 7,000 were left. In the mid-'80s, the order to scrap them altogether was passed. Steam engines were slowly shunted from main trunk lines to remote branch lines and ultimately to locomotive graveyards. Most have been sold off as scrap and only about 400 are left now.

All that remains are fond memories of the chugging, whistling dame. Each steam loco had its own nuances and sounds. Drivers and firemen would learn to feel the pulse of the loco by her sound and hissing. When they took their engines for their last run, many of them, heartbroken, cried.

Though the global revival of steam began in the 1970s, it took India almost thirty years to recognise steam engines. In 1997, *Fairy Queen* – which runs every winter from Delhi to Alwar – was put back on the track. It was not until 1999 that the HGS 26761 at Howrah and *Baby Sivok* on the Darjeeling Himalayan Railway (DHR)

In 1853, *Sindh* of GIPR worked the inaugral train.

were revived. Thereafter, North East Frontier Railway has resurrected the MAWD 1798 – it takes tourists down the Brahmaputra near Guwahati – and a YG – in charge of Jatinga Steam Safari in the breathtaking Lumding Halflong Hill section of Assam. DHR was accorded World Heritage status by UNESCO in December 1999. A DHR engine has also been readied for the Neral Matheran, 2-ft gauge system, while the KC 520 *Pawan Doot* will chug the blue slopes on the Kalka-Shimla Railway. The National Rail Museum has three WP-class locomotives that are often used by film-makers – one of these features in the Hindi movie, *Gadar*.

Though most steam engines have been phased out, old-timers retain their nostalgia . . . the sweet smell of smoke wafting into the carriages, the coal bits in the hair, the chug and whistle and the clickety-clack of the train over the tracks . . . The irresistible poetry of steam will not be easily forgotten. Hopefully . . .

■ The *Fairy* is cleaned up at Alwar

Fairy Queen is the oldest preserved steam locomotive in the country and figures in the *Guinness Book* as the oldest working steam locomotive in the world. It was manufactured by Kiston, Hewitson & Thomson, Leeds, UK in 1885. Its sister, the Express, hauled the first passenger train which steamed out of Howrah for Hoogly, a distance of 24 miles, on 15 August 1854. She also hauled troop trains to Raniganj during the famous War of Independence in 1857. She hauls a heritage special every winter from Delhi to Alwar.

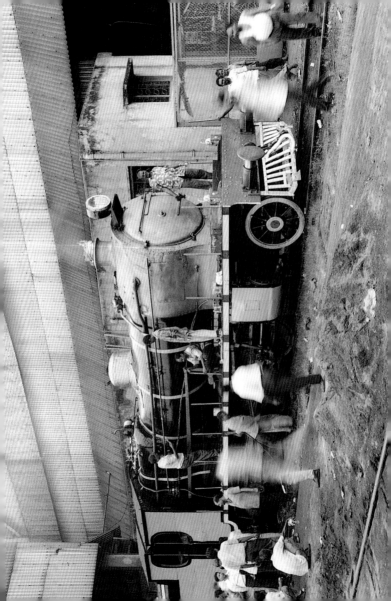

■ The Heavy Goods Superheated locomotive 26761 is spruced up at the Howrah shed.

The HGS (Heavy Goods Superheated) 26761 broad gauge locomotive was manufactured by W. M. Beardmore Company, England, and commissioned in 1922. This locomotive initially worked under the Oudh and Rohilkhund Railway (O&RR), and then operated in Eastern Railway's Asansol division till 1985. It was then sent for maintenance at the Madhupur locomotive shed in Bihar.

■ The WP 7015 is shunted out of the Dehradun shed for the Doon Railway Centenary.

This powerful broad gauge steam locomotive is India's glory in steam locomotives. Called the WP in the coding system of the railways – which signifies that it is a broad gauge passenger – it was pressed into service in 1947 and pulled most prestigious passenger trains. With a wheel structure of 4-6-2 and a driving wheel size of 67 in, the WP can haul up to 16 coaches and is typified by the star painted on its nose. The WP 7015 was manufactured in 1959 at Charznow, Poland. The last WP locomotive was made in 1967 at Chitranjan Locomotive Works, Bengal.

■ One of the last working broad gauge American War Engines in the world hauls a coal rake at Korba.

Pre-independence India, an American ally, got hundreds of 'War Department' locomotives to alleviate the prevailing motive power shortage. The AWE (American War Engine) was one of three such 'War Department' class locomotives supplied to India, the other two classes being the Canadian broad gauge and the Meter Gauge American War Department (MAWD). The AWE was built by the Baldwin Locomotive Works, Philadelphia, the premier locomotive builder in the US. In India, it was used for hauling heavy mineral trains.

■ The AWE 3315 speeds out of the shed after a paint job at Korba, Chattisgarh.

The vast capacity of the American locomotive industry resulted in thousands of locomotives being built for war service during the 1939-1945 period. Even before the Pearl Harbour disaster, locomotives were being built to order for the British Government under the 'lease-lend' arrangements then in force. Several American War Engines (AWE) were used for hauling heavy mineral trains and slower passenger services like the Toofan Mail.

■ A Meter Gauge American War Department (MAWD) train steams up in Guwahati.

The Meter Gauge American War Department locomotives (MAWD) were built by the Baldwin Locomotive Works, USA. They were popularly also known as Mac Arthur, after the famous American general of World War II.

■ The MAWD 1798, rebuilt by North East Frontier Railway, runs tourist specials in Assam.

With their stovepipe chimneys and bar frames, the MAWDs were typical American locomotives with a wheel arrangement of 2-8-2 (Pony Couple Radial). Though these engines were designed and built in a hurry, they rendered yeoman service to the railways which owned them long after the War had ended.

■ *Brahmaputra by Steam* is a heritage special pulled by the MAWD 1798 from Guwahati to Pandu.

The MAWD 1798 was manufactured by Baldwin Locomotive Works, Philadelphia, USA in 1944. It was put to service on Indian tracks in 1944. The last passenger service run by this locomotive in the Alipurduar–Gitaldah section was in 1993. MAWD class locomotives have a coal capacity of 8.12 tonnes, and can drink up to 10,000 gallons of water.

■ Jama Jiva, a fitter at the Wankaner shed, Gujarat

The Indian Railway is probably the largest employer in the world. The Railway's success is due to the effort, commitment and passion of its railwaymen. After the end of the steam era in the 1970s and 1980s, hundreds of steam mechanics, drivers, fitters and foremen were left floundering. To preserve the skills that these people have would be India's greatest tribute to its railway heritage.

■ The locomotive shed at Mettupalayam with the Nilgiris in the background

The 46-km metre gauge line connecting Udgamandalam (Ooty) to Mettupalayam is under the Nilgiri Mountain Railway (NMR). Its first section up to Conoor was completed in 1899 at a cost of Rs 59 lakh. It served as a getaway from the sweltering heat of the plains for the British in India. Even today it is a popular hill resort.

■ A steam locomotive is steel all the way, its visible moving parts giving it great beauty.

Since 1899, steam locomotives have been the motive power on the Nilgiri Mountain Railway. All traffic on the rack section is in the able hands of eight X-class locomotives. These are compound locomotives having four cylinders instead of the conventional two. The main cylinders use high-pressure steam and drive the wheels while the smaller cylinders use low-pressure steam to drive the rack system. The youngest X-class is over fifty years old and the oldest is seventy-five years old as against the average twenty-five-year working life of a steam locomotive.

■ The 37386 X-class rack locomotive hisses at Mettupalayam during shunting.

Of all the steam railways, David Lean chose the NMR to become Chandrapore Railway in his film, A Passage to India. Then we have Rishi Kapoor in Zamane Ko Dikhana Hai, K. Balachandar's Sadma and Mani Ratnam in Dil. The last brought out the essence of the NMR as actors Shahrukh Khan and Malaika sashayed on top of the train to the tunes of Chaiya Chaiya.

■ The workshop at Mettupalayam

Snaking through 208 hairpin bends, 76 lubricating points and across 249 bridges and 16 tunnels cutting across the mountain sides, the Nilgiri trains chug on their romantic journey. The steam engine with its four passenger coaches stops at eight places for water.

■ Thirteen men and the 804 B at New Jalpaiguri

Fourteen B class, 2-ft narrow gauge steam locomotives keep the Darjeeling Himalayan Railway (DHR) alive. The line that was commissioned in 1881 was accorded World Heritage status by the UNESCO in 1999.

■ A train struggles up the slope at Batasia in the backdrop of a dream house.

The first locomotives on the Darjeeling Himalayan Railway (DHR) line were the C class tank types but these were quickly withdrawn in favour of the more powerful A class well tanks. Finally, the world famous B class Saddle Tanks emerged in 1888.

■ The Ghum railway station retains its old style.

The DHR from New Jalpaiguri (NJP) covers a distance of 88 km. It has about 150 unmanned level crossings and a ruling gradient of 1:22½. It rises from 373 feet at NJP to its summit of 7,407 feet at Ghum.

■ Women lead a procession for Free Tibet in Sonada as a UP train waits at the station.

Liveries of locomotives on the DHR have varied over the years. The engines were originally painted olive green although during World War II they were made black. Between 1952 and 57, brick-red livery was adopted. Since 1958, blue has become the symbol of the B class DHR locomotives.

■ Girls watch an engine shunt in thick fog at Tindharia.

The Darjeeling Himalayan Railway serves as a transport medium for numerous school children living along the track. The trains are so slow that it is convenient for children to get on and off as they please. In fact, the passenger train from Kurseong to Darjeeling is fondly called the School Train.

■ Loco foreman Nal Bahadur stands with his engine.

About 865 men and women work to make the Darjeeling Himalayan Railway run. Among them are drivers, mechanics, engineers, foremen, fitters, clerks, and cleaners. Their dedication and commitment to keep the railway chugging has been exemplary.

■ The Batasia Loop on the Darjeeling Himalayan Railway

To overcome the steep gradient on the line, the DHR uses 'loops'. Here the line is able to climb at a less acute gradient by means of a spiral ascent crossing itself at a higher altitude. There are three loops in all, the tightest one being the Bismail Loop, also called Agony Point.

■ The *Baby Sivok* and the 804 B begin a fresh day.

A fascinating feature of the Darjeeling Himalayan Railway's steam locomotive operations is the number of crew required – five. In addition to the driver and fireman, there is a coal-breaker who sits on top of the tiny engine and two men who sit in front of the locomotive to do the sanding.

■ The Ghum Special is pulled by the oldest locomotive today, the 779 B built in 1892.

Darjeeling is the destination of the 88-km line. The art deco style of the the 1940s Darjeeling station (right) is now submerged by the rectangular stories added later (left), whilst the English-style church on the right also demonstrates the early building style.

■ At Tipong in remote Upper Assam, an ex-DHR locomotive hauls coal wagons.

A large number of industries all over India also used steam locomotives. The railway was first used in India in 1851 when Thomason (a standard gauge steam engine) started work for the construction of the Solani aqueduct, 125 km from Delhi. This was two years before the first passenger train ran between Bombay and Thane in 1853. Today only a few industrial steam engines remain.

■ The coal train at Tipong colliery

Locomotives used by industry were mostly bought from the Indian Railways. Steel plants, cement factories, sugar mills, collieries, power plants, aluminum factories, brick works – all used steam engines for transporting their raw materials. Three major ports in India – Bombay Port Trust, Calcutta Port and Madras Port – used a large number of steam locomotives. Sugar mills in Bihar and Uttar Pradesh still have a few working steam engines.

■ *Front cover:* The Darjeeling train struggles up to Batasia in heavy fog.
■ *Page 2:* Men work on the 804 B at New Jalpaiguri.
■ *Page 3:* The train approaches the Batasia Loop from Darjeeling.
■ *Back cover:* Black magic beyond the wall, Wankaner